TWELVE SMALL WINDOWS

TWELVE SMALL WINDOWS
Short Poems for Seeing Clearly

by J. A. Gucci
Teacher Edition

Pressure System Press
NewYork, New York

2026

TWELVE SMALL WINDOWS (Teacher Edition)
© 2026 J. A. Gucci
All rights reserved.

No part of this publication may be reproduced, stored in a retrieval system, or transmitted in any form or by any means — electronic, mechanical, photocopying, recording, or otherwise — without the prior written permission of the publisher, except in the case of brief quotations used for review or educational purposes.

Published by Pressure System Press
Brooklyn, New York

ISBN: 979-8-9946751-5-1

Printed in the United States of America

First Edition, 2026

www.jagucci.com

Dedication

For the teachers
who show students
how to see what's there—
and what loops beneath.

Table of Contents

Author's Note 9
How to Use This Book 11
About the Paradox Triads 13

Oxbow Lake 17
Frost Heave 19
The Silent Train 21
Re-calibration 23
Experience 25
Projection 27
Flicker 29
Leather Foot 31
Resilience 33
Messy Cycle 35
Ship of Theseus 37
Again, Moon 39

Glossary 41
Student Prompts 43

Author's Note

Twelve Small Windows is built on a simple belief: students learn to write by noticing.

Each "window" in this book focuses attention on one manageable element of writing—image, sound, detail, perspective, memory, or structure. The goal is not to overwhelm students with technique, but to help them look closely at one thing at a time.

Middle school writers benefit from clear frames. A window provides that frame. It narrows the field so students can practice precision without feeling lost.

Teachers are encouraged to move flexibly. A window may open for a single class period or remain open for several days. Revisit earlier windows as needed. Growth at this age is rarely linear.

Writing improves when students feel safe enough to try, notice, adjust, and try again.

This book is designed to make that process visible.

How to Use This Book

This book is built for flexibility. There is no fixed order, no prerequisite knowledge, and no need for extended background lectures.

Each poem follows a paradox triad — three words that form a loop of tension, transformation, or return. These paradoxes are not explained in the poems. That's intentional. Students are invited to notice patterns, not decode meaning.

Each poem is paired with a classroom page that includes discussion prompts, writing tasks, and observation notes.

Suggested Use:

- **One poem per week**
  Read aloud. Project it. Give time for silence. Ask: What do you see? What changed? What loop did it follow?

- **Triad Discussions**
  Introduce the paradox after the poem. Ask: How do these three ideas live inside the poem?

- **Student Writing**
  Invite students to build their own triads. Write short poems rooted in real-world phenomena. No metaphors. No symbols. Just observation under pressure.

- **Cross-Disciplinary Connections**
  Encourage links to science (systems, cycles), visual art (composition, negative space), and music (tension, resolution, variation).

Assessment (if needed):

- Can the student describe a system or process in the poem?
- Can the student write a short, image-based poem with clear structure?
- Can the student identify the paradox loop, even intuitively?

This book teaches compression, attention, and clarity — skills that matter far beyond poetry.

About the Paradox Triads

At the heart of each poem in this book is a paradox triad: a set of three words that resist easy explanation — yet clearly describe how something changes, fractures, returns, or evolves.

The words are not symbolic. They aren't chosen for emotion. They are chosen for tension.

Each triad creates a loop.
Each loop becomes a form.
Each form becomes a poem.

These are not just writing prompts — they are structural engines. They teach students how to:

- Work within constraints
- Observe natural systems
- Express contradiction without abstraction
- Let meaning emerge from form, not flourish

Why paradox?

Middle school students are already living paradox:
They want to be seen and hidden.
They want control and release.
They feel old and young.

These poems help them hold those tensions without needing to resolve them.

Sample Triads:

- Crack / Ice / Water → transformation under pressure

- Noise / Echo / Silence → space and memory

- Map / Path / Lost → direction and disorientation

- Same / Again / Strange → repetition with difference

Students can also generate their own — and in doing so, begin to recognize that even complexity can have shape.

*We return not to repeat,
but to understand.*

Classroom Guide

Poem: Oxbow Lake
Triad: Start / Middle / Gone
Loop Theme: Time as motion and vanishing

Think It Through:
- What broke the river's path?
- Where is the "start"? Where is the "gone"?
- What does the lily mean if nothing is left of the stream?

Try It Yourself:
Write about something that used to move — but doesn't anymore.
Keep it simple. Use only images. Don't explain.

Observe This:
Look up how oxbow lakes form.
It takes hundreds of turns to make one perfect curve.

Oxbow Lake

Sun,
snow,
a mountain—
dripping,

streams rippling,
river chipping,
a bank breaks—

a lily blooms.

For the Classroom

Poem: Frost Heave
Triad: Crack / Ice / Water
Loop Theme: Transformation under pressure

Think It Through:
- What causes the crack?
- What happens when water changes form?
- What's the relationship between damage and weather?

Try It Yourself:
Write a poem where something invisible causes something loud.
Keep it physical. Keep it short.

Observe This:
Search "frost heave" or "alligator cracking."
These are signs of change underground.

Frost Heave

Afternoon rain—
seeping,

dusk—
frozen water
swelling,

alligator cracking—
pothole.

For the Classroom

Poem: The Silent Train
Triad: Noise / Echo / Silence
Loop Theme: Sound, space, and what's left

Think It Through:
- What makes the silence louder than the sound?
- How is the train present even after it's gone?
- What does the ground remember?

Try It Yourself:
Write a poem where sound leaves a shape.
Use verbs that carry movement and impact.

Observe This:
Some trains have ditch lights angled outward to sweep the tracks.
They arrive before the sound does.

The Silent Train

Ditch light—
loom—
billows and swirls,

low hum—
screeching steel on steel—
a shifting shaking ground—

a quiet roar,
footsteps on stairs.

For the Classroom

Poem: Re-calibration
Triad: Flock / One / Lost
Loop Theme: Belonging, straying, identity

Think It Through:
- What happened to the juvenile starling?
- What does it mean to be "adrift" in a group?
- What does the flock know that the one doesn't?

Try It Yourself:
Write about something that strays from its system. Let the poem drift, then land.

Observe This:
Starlings move in murmurations — massive, synchronized shapes.
But even one bird, off-course, still carries the pattern inside.

Re-calibration

Starlings soaring through sky—
a tear drop.

Gust of wind—
a juvenile
astride,
astray—

adrift…

For the Classroom

Poem: Experience
Triad: Mistake / Pattern / Memory
Loop Theme: Order from error

Think It Through:
- What changed between the first and last stanza?
- How does the middle stanza act as a memory?
- What pattern does the "hot stove" create?

Try It Yourself:
Write about a moment where something painful became useful.
Use repetition to show a lesson forming.

Observe This:
Skin regenerates in layers after a burn.
Mistakes leave traces — sometimes protection.

Experience

Hot stove:
red glow,
shimmering air,

shiny bubbles pop—
crust-dried,
smooth hands.

Hot stove:
red glow—
oven mitts.

For the Classroom

Poem: Projection
Triad: Shadow / Shape / Sun
Loop Theme: Identity through contrast

Think It Through:
- How do the shadows change throughout the day?
- Which shadow feels more accurate — the small one or the long one?
- What does light reveal that shape alone cannot?

Try It Yourself:
Write a poem about something that changes size without changing itself.
Keep your language physical. Let contrast do the work.

Observe This:
At midday, your shadow shrinks.
At dusk, it stretches past you — an outline out of scale.

Projection

Zenith—
gleaming—
my tiny shadow
under feet.

Level,
pale—
my long shadow
on the wall.

For the Classroom

Poem: Flicker
Triad: Real / Dream / Wake
Loop Theme: Slippage between states

Think It Through:
- What changes in the cuttlefish between sleep and waking?
- How do we know what's real if both states have color and motion?
- Where is the "loop" in this transformation?

Try It Yourself:
Write a poem where something imagined prepares you for something real.
Let the shift be quiet. Let it flicker.

Observe This:
Cuttlefish change color when dreaming — their bodies react to imagined worlds.
Then they shift again when they wake.

Flicker

A crimson cuttlefish,
asleep—
dreaming:

salmon skin—
yellow,
now green,
blue.

A blink—
crimson cuttlefish—
awake.

For the Classroom

Poem: Leather Foot
Triad: Map / Path / Lost
Loop Theme: Direction, decision, disorientation

Think It Through:
- Why does the ant's journey change when the foot appears?
- What's the difference between a path and a map?
- Can you be "lost" even when heading home?

Try It Yourself:
Write a poem where something interrupts a familiar route.
Use distance, speed, or scale to show the change.

Observe This:
Ants leave scent trails — a kind of invisible map.
When disrupted, they improvise.

Leather Foot

Ant on rye—
streaking to nest—
long and windy.

Leather foot over sidewalk—
a scout scurries astray,

streaking to nest—
short and straight.

For the Classroom

Poem: Resilience
Triad: Hold / Drop / Change
Loop Theme: Control, release, transformation

Think It Through:
- What does the snake have to give up to grow?
- How does the image of the sock "inside out" help us understand the process?
- What is being held? What is being shed?

Try It Yourself:
Write a poem where something becomes new by letting go.
Use texture and detail — make it feel like touch.

Observe This:
Before shedding, a snake's eyes cloud over.
The old skin pulls away — but only after a break.

Resilience

Milk eyes,
undulating snout—

a sock—
inside out.

Dead skin—
glistening.

For the Classroom

Poem: Messy Cycle
Triad: Rain / Mud / Bloom
Loop Theme: Cycles of growth

Think It Through:
- What's "messy" about this version of growth?
- How do the colors change from stanza to stanza?
- Why end with the lotus?

Try It Yourself:
Write a poem where something beautiful grows from something foul.
Don't explain the change — just show it.

Observe This:
The sacred lotus grows in mud.
Its petals stay dry. Its roots stay deep.

Messy Cycle

Rain—

sickly bruised
charcoal gray,

streaks of oil,
trapped gases,

swampy olive patches,
rotting wood—

Sacred Lotus.

For the Classroom

Poem: Ship of Theseus
Triad: Gone / Back / Different
Loop Theme: Return with residue

Think It Through:
- What parts of the tree are "gone," and which return in new form?
- How does the transformation happen over time?
- What makes something the "same" if every part of it has changed?

Try It Yourself:
Write a poem about something that comes back changed.
Use clear steps, like a chain reaction — but stay rooted in the physical.

Observe This:
The Ship of Theseus is a thought experiment:
If every part of a thing is replaced, is it still the same thing?

Ship of Theseus

Bare branches—
snap,

sap—
frozen,
welling—

shivering wax bulbs
wobbling—
neon chartreuse,

engorged leaves,
bursting.

Dew—
sweet astringent air.

For the Classroom

Poem: Again, Moon
Triad: Same / Again / Strange
Loop Theme: Repetition with shift

Think It Through:
- What repeats in the poem? What changes?
- How is the moon both constant and altered by the ripple?
- Is the "again" comforting, or unsettling?

Try It Yourself:
Write a poem where the same image appears twice but feels different the second time.

Observe This:
The moon's reflection changes with every ripple. It's still the moon — but not quite the same.

Again, Moon

Glimmering
glass lake,

a stone—
ripples—

shivering moon.

Glossary

A brief reference for scientific and technical words in the poems.

Alligator Cracking – A type of pavement fracture that resembles reptile skin, caused by swelling and pressure underneath. Seen in roads during freeze-thaw cycles.

Cuttlefish – A marine animal related to the octopus that can change its skin color and texture. They also change colors while dreaming.

Ditch Light – A pair of lights on the front of a train, angled to sweep the tracks ahead. Used to warn animals and vehicles.

Frost Heave – The upward swelling of soil during freezing conditions, caused by the expansion of moisture underground.

Lotus – A flower that grows in muddy water. Sacred in many cultures. Its petals stay clean despite its murky environment.

Murmuration – A large, shifting flock of starlings flying in coordinated patterns.

Oxbow Lake – A curved lake formed when a river changes course and cuts off one of its old loops.

Paradox Triad – A set of three words that seem to contradict, but together form a poetic structure. Each poem in this book is based on one.

Projection (Shadow) – The way light creates distorted versions of an object depending on time and angle.

Resilience – The ability to recover, adapt, or grow stronger after being changed or harmed.

Student Writing Prompts

Ways to help students create their own "small windows."

These prompts follow the same method as the poems in this book:
Start with what's real. Keep it physical. Let the structure reveal meaning.

1. Write a Triad Poem
Choose three words that describe change, contradiction, or return.
Examples: crack / repair / scar, or push / float / sink.

Now write a short poem that shows those words happening — without naming them.

2. Show the System
Pick a natural process:
a snake shedding, a leaf falling, a puddle evaporating.
Write it in three stanzas:

- What starts
- What shifts
- What's left

3. Remove the I
Write a poem with no "I," "me," or "my."
Let the world do the speaking.
Show what happens — not how you feel about it.

4. Echo One
Pick your favorite poem from this book.
Now write a new version — same triad, new system.

5. Reverse It
Write a triad poem backward.
Start with what's left.
End with where it came from.

The Twelve Series

Each book in this series presents systems through short, structured poems.

Rather than describing events, the poems model how systems form, interact, and change over time.

Each volume focuses on a different civilization, using the same method to reveal how complex societies develop.

History

Mesopotamia — Formation
Greece — Interaction
Rome — Expansion and Collapse
Medieval — Thresholds

Creative Writing

Twelve Loops
Twelve Mirrors
Twelve Rooms

Philosophy

Twelve Iron Paradoxes

About the Author

J. A. Gucci is a poet, composer, and educator. He has written over a dozen books exploring how form, observation, and contradiction shape meaning.

He believes poetry doesn't need metaphor to be powerful — just attention, precision, and patience.

He has taught composition and creative process to students from elementary school to university, and continues to explore how thinking clearly and looking closely can change how we create.

This is his first book written especially for middle school readers.

www.ingramcontent.com/pod-product-compliance
Lightning Source LLC
LaVergne TN
LVHW041641070526
838199LV00052B/3486